MOTHERS
AND DAUGHTERS

First published by Parragon in 2011

Parragon
Queen Street House
4 Queen Street
Bath BA1 1HE, UK

Copyright © Parragon Books Ltd 2011
Design by Pink Creative Ltd

ISBN: 978-1-4454-4341-6

Printed in China

MOTHERS
AND DAUGHTERS
SHARED WISDOM FROM ME TO YOU

PaRragon

Bath • New York • Singapore • Hong Kong • Cologne • Delhi
Melbourne • Amsterdam • Johannesburg • Auckland • Shenzhen

Children need love, especially when they do not deserve it.

Harold Hulbert

Over my slumbers your loving watch keep; Rock me to sleep, mother, rock me to sleep.

Elizabeth Chase

A mother is she

who can take

the place

of all others

but whose place

no one else

can take.

Cardinal Mermillod

Our daughters are the most precious of our treasures, the dearest possessions of our homes and the objects of our most watchful love.

Margaret E. Sangster

Of all the rights of
women,
the greatest is to be a
mother.

Lin Yutang

My favourite place to be
is inside of your hugs
where it's warm and loving.

Anonymous

A little girl, asked where her home was, replied, "where mother is."

Keith L. Brooks

Some are kissing mothers and some are scolding mothers, but it is love just the same and most mothers kiss and scold together.

Pearl S. Buck

Beloved,
you are my sister,
you are my daughter, you
are my face; you are me.

Toni Morrison

A mother is
the truest
friend we have.

Washington Irving

What do girls do who haven't any mothers to help them through their troubles?

Louisa May Alcott

God couldn't be
everywhere, so
he created mothers.

Jewish Proverb

Motherhood:

All love begins and ends there.

Robert Browning

A mother's
treasure
is her daughter.

Catherine Pulsifer

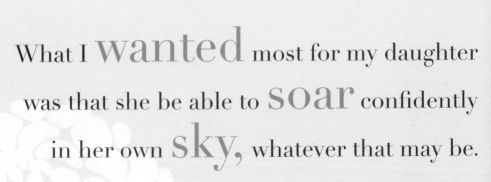

What I wanted most for my daughter was that she be able to soar confidently in her own sky, whatever that may be.

Helen Claes

What the daughter **does,** the mother **did.**

Jewish Proverb

I am **fond**
of children –
except boys.

Lewis Carroll

My mother by chance, my friend by choice.

Anonymous

Children make you want

to start life over.

Muhammad Ali

A daughter may outgrow your lap,
but she will never outgrow your heart.

Anonymous

Who fed me from her gentle breast,
And hushed me in her arms to rest,
And on my cheek sweet kisses prest?
My Mother

Anne Taylor

A daughter is a little girl
who grows up
to be a friend.

Anonymous

We worry about what a child will become tomorrow, yet we forget that she is someone today.

Stacia Tauscher

48

Mothers hold
their daughters hand
a little while and their
hearts forever.

Anonymous

Mother: the most
beautiful
word on the lips of
mankind.

Kahlil Gibran

My mom is a never-ending song in my heart.

Graycie Harmon

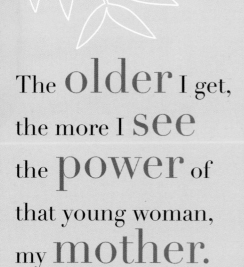

The older I get,
the more I see
the power of
that young woman,
my mother.

Sharon Olds

A daughter is one of the most beautiful gifts this world has to give.

Laurel Atherton

A daughter is a day
brightener

and a heart
warmer.

Anonymous

A child can ask questions that a wise man cannot answer.

Anonymous

A **mother** is one to
whom you **turn** when
you are **troubled**.

Emily Dickinson

A mother's love for her child
is like nothing else
in the world.
Agatha Christie

All that I am,
or hope to be,
I owe to my
angel mother.

Abraham Lincoln

A mother
understands
what a child does not say.

Jewish Proverb

Daughters are angels sent from above

to fill our heart with **unending** love.

Anonymous

The heart of a mother is a deep abyss at the bottom of which you will always find forgiveness.

Honoré de Balzac

Even when freshly washed

and relieved of all obvious

confections,

children tend to be sticky.

Fran Lebowitz

No gift to your mother
can ever equal
her gift to you – life.

Anonymous

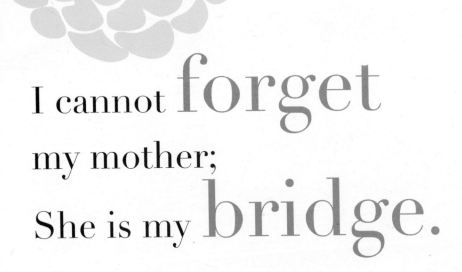

I cannot forget my mother; She is my bridge.

Renita Weems

A daughter is the happy memories of the past, the joyful moments of the present, and the hope and promise of the future.

Anonymous

Mothers of daughters are daughters of mothers and have remained so, in circles joined to circles, since time began.

Signe Hammer

The only thing worth stealing is a kiss from a sleeping child.

Joe Houldsworth

Mothers and daughters
are closest,

when daughters

become mothers.

Anonymous

Mother's love is peace. It need not be acquired, it need not be deserved.

Erich Fromm

She's my teacher,
my advisor,
my greatest
inspiration.

Anonymous

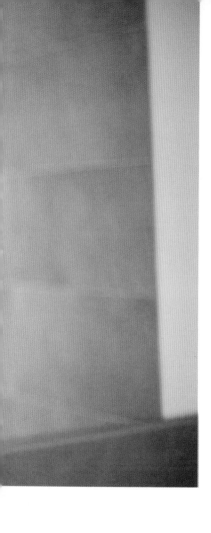

Like Mother, like Daughter.

Proverb

Picture credits